Stephanie Aird

I Bring To You...

This book is dedicated to all
my **Phannies,**
Thank you so much for all
of your continued support.

love, Stephanie x

This is soooooo exciting, right, where the fuck do I start.................................
Oooh I know-a contents page, yaaaaay.

Awww yeah and if you spot any spelling or grammer mistakes, they're on purpose just to keep you on your toes!!! Honestly, they are.........

Contents

Secrets, Revelations and Other TitBits

Chapter 1

A little bit about me, Stephanie.....
Many of you know me from my Facebook and YouTube comedy videos. I am so excited to publish my first ever book! I want to thank each one of my Phannies for all the continuing support I have had from you, it really means a lot to me.

<u>Briefly In the beginning</u> - I was born in Lambeth, London on 4th October 1968. Ever since I was about 8 years old I had a dream, the dream was that I wanted to be a musician/artist/entertainer.

<u>Briefly In the middle</u> - In 1990 I had my first daughter, yaaaay and in 1997 I had my second daughter, yaaaay (I counted the 'a's in both yaaaays 'cos I know bloody nicely they both will). I also went to college and university during those years and in 1997 as well as having my second daughter I started working as a teacher and continued to do so for 18 years until I got suspended in 2014 for making inappropriate videos.

<u>Briefly more recently</u> - Eventually I left my job and continued making Facebook videos. My fan base has grown at an amazing rate. Right now I have 125,000 Facebook Fans and 5,000 YouTube Subscribers, which is absolutely unbelievable, I never dreamed of coming anywhere near that. At the start of 2016 I had about 7,000 Facebook Fans, which then boosted to 45,000 in September and now to 125,000 in December. I love meeting my Phannies and whenever I go out and about there are always people who know who I am, eee it's like being a celebrity, rich and famous without the rich bit.

<u>Briefly now</u> – as well as being a megastar (ish) I am also an owner of a cafe-bar which is called 'Stephanie's Cafe-Bar-Shoppe'
55 Church Street, Hartlepool!!!!

It is mad to think that when the cafe-bar first opened hardly anyone was visiting and now I have reached out to many more people, I am having sell out shows and nights of a packed out bar of people who visit to see me and of course poor Ian, its bloody amazing.

I have written poetry and songs ever since I was about 8 years old. I love words and melodies and find excitement in putting them together. I am proud to say that I have had over 25 of my songs/instrumental pieces played on BBC Introducing and other Radio stations. I write, perform, record, edit and master all of my own tracks, usually at home or sometimes at my caravan. I have also composed many pieces when on holiday. Most of my songs and albums are on iTunes, YouTube, Reverbnation and Soundcloud. I also design and make physical CDs which I sell as merch at my gigs, shows and at my Cafe-Bar-Shoppe (55 Church, Street, Hartlepool).

I've include some of my lyrics in the book but be warned,.....my lyrics can be quite dark at times in contrast to my comedy videos.

Although on the whole I try to create beautiful, heartfelt and poignant messages through my music.

As some of you may know, I have 2 albums out. Yaaaaaaay-In September 2016 my debut single 'Bricking Up The Bridges' was released on iTunes, Google Play and Amazon Music. Up to now the single has shown huge success. My 2nd single 'Relentless' was released in October 2016 also showing success. This I am really thankful for and I am so happy that people enjoy my music.

Chapter 2

I'm also a tourer... Or is it traveller...
In November of 2016, I announced my first
ever tour dates, one being in Billingham and
one in Norton. By late November my
Billingham gig had SOLD OUT! And by the 2nd
week in December my Norton show had SOLD
OUT too! I was overwhelmed, over the moon
and under the table (tad too much celebratory
Cava Ma' Darlings).

On Friday 2nd December 2016, I had my first
ever tour date at The Swan Hotel Billingham.
Over 220 people turned out to see the show. I
had many surprises for the fans that had come
to see me. As I was about to go on stage, I felt
petrified, The lights went down, I walked out
on stage not showing any sign of being scared.
I instantly felt a connection with my fans. The
crowd were so friendly, apart from one bloke
heckling me, I soon shut him up, the smart
arse!!! The show turned out to be amazing and
everyone loved it! At the end of the show I had
one person ask me for a selfie, once I said yes,
there was a line right to the back of the
theatre of people wanting selfies and
signatures. I can't believe how many people
actually wanted to meet me, again I felt like a
celebrity, yaaaay!

As soon as the queue disappeared and everyone had a selfie, I went backstage and that was it..... It was over. All the hard work, rehearsals and dedication paid off. As soon as my excitement had died down a little me and Ian got in our little Citroen and drove home. I couldn't sleep for excitement and I couldn't stop thinking about the Norton show exactly 1 week after that day. Thank you to anybody who bought a ticket or has showed any kind of support to me over the past 2 years, YOUS are friggin' MINT!

I have been working on some brilliant projects in this past year. I have met some truly amazing, kind people who have helped me with a lot of things I wanted to achieve. Without these people I wouldn't have been able to achieve many of the things I've achieved. Well I would of it just would have taken me a tad longer ma' darlings!!!

In 2017 I will carry on writing songs, produce a new album, have more tour dates, hopefully sell outs and get the opportunity to be in panto and sitcoms, I've been cast in an exciting new sitcom – EXTRA EXTRA set in Liverpool, yaaaay. The thing I love the most is making people laugh and when I see that I have helped someone get through a rough patch in their life, it really cheers me up. I love seeing lovely comments from my Phannies, it helps me become more successful in life, without some of your comments I wouldn't have had the courage to carry on making my videos, writing music and go on tour.

The Videos

A Selection Transcribed

Tesco Direct

"Morning, I'm sorry I didn't report to you yesterday about my Tesco delivery, I was too upset, and sorry about my red eyes, I've been up crying all night. What it was, I ordered a dingy and two life jackets on Tesco Direct, I thought it was amazing because you can order like these items and they'd deliver them to your local Express, and we've got one just round the corner, so I thought it was like really mint. So anyway I ordered them, cause' I wanted them for the raft race today, and they come yesterday and I had to pick them up between 4 and 6pm. So I went round, I was all excited, and when I got there like I had a slip thing like on my phone cause' I couldn't print it off and you have to have like an invoice number and I took a screenshot of it and it was on my phone, cause' it was an email from Tesco. And anyway I went in and I went to the man and I said 'Can I have my delivery please' and he said 'Oh yeah, it's come out the back' well I swear to God I was so excited. Anyway he went out the back and he come with like a plastic bag, which I could see were the life jackets, I could just see, you can just tell cant you by the shape of a package what it is, and a box, like a really big box, and I thought well, it said its a compact dingy, that you can like deflate and put away for easy storage, so I thought it was a really big box.

Anyway he brought them down and he says 'Here is your packages' and he read it off the sheets, he said 'two life jackets and a set of wicker drawers.' I said 'I didn't order that, a set of wicker drawers' I said 'I ordered some life jackets and a dingy for the raft race' he said 'Are you sure?' I said 'Yeah, yeah I'm sure yeah' and there was like a queue of people and they all looked at him, and he said 'Are you positive?' And they all looked at me, waiting for my answer, as if I could have got the order wrong. Who'd order two life jackets and a set of wicker drawers? The life jackets nice like, isn't it? It's all right. Anyway I said 'I don't want the wicker drawers'he said 'you have to take them; I had to go and get Ian out the car to sort it out. To be honest they were nice like and they would've looked lovely on the landing upstairs, but Ian said 'No Stephanie, no you don't need any more drawers' anyway I don't know what I'm going to do about the raft race today. If anybody has a space on one of your rafts can I come on please? Thank you bye."

Stephanie Aird-12K Views

Trolls Think Before Ya Type

"Morning, It's me again, I've put my chuddy in for this. My mini manager Callum, bless him, has just sent me some screenshots of people having a go about the price of my calendar. Well bare this in mind; they said "Well Michael Buble's is only 8 pounds" Right Ok. Michael Buble is a multimillionaire and probably sells millions of calendars, I ordered 20... 20, not 20 million, 20. These calendars cost me... with the printing, the packaging, the petrol to take them right the way down the post office and everything all in, the calendars cost me about £12.50 each, and I'm selling them all in for £15, so I'm making about £2.50 per calendar, and I've sold 20. So what have I made there? 10 x £2.50... 50 quid, actually it cost me £40 for the photo shoot for them, so there's £40 off that... there a tenner I've made, a tenner. It took me three hours to cut the cardboard out and pack them, so a tenner divided by three, £3 per hour, minimum wage is what? £8, £7 odd, so I'm working at half the minimum wage, so don't have a go at me at the price of the calendars, if Michael Buble's is cheaper buy his fucking calendar, not arsed. Honestly.
In fact I might go and get a Michael Buble calendar, I do like a bit of Buble, I really, really do. Bye"

Stephanie Aird-26.4k views

My run in with Donald Trump

S "Hello, are you on? Hiya, I bring to you... I'm gonna try a different sandwich today, I'm gonna try Tesco's, nothing wrong with Boots'but I thought I'd mix it up a bit, you know I like to mix it up. 249 calories, that's not bad is it? Fucking hell there's an old gadgie at the window do I wind it down? I'm a woman on my own. God what does he want? Hello?"

D "I'm very sorry but you can't park here this is my land, it's my land, also I've seen your car and I realised you have a cafe-bar, which is 55 Church Street, Hartlepool, I really want to buy that, I want to buy that off you, if that's Ok... put me in an offer, I want an offer. I'll tell you what, I'll give you a million dollars for your cafe-shoppe-bar cause I can make that even more successful than a lot of my businesses cause this is all my business, all these houses around here, this is all my work people are building around here, see those over there? They're my cows, my private jet is parked in the cow field over there, I want to buy your business off you, I want to buy your business Stephanie"

S "How do you know my name?"

D "Because I've seen your videos, I think they're fantastic, when you walk on and say, "Hello, I bring to you... Ian is doing my fucking head in" and all those type of things, I'm sure your husband is not very happy about that, but I find them very funny, and I'm so glad that I've caught you eating a sandwich in my area"

S "Do you want some? Cause I've just opened it"

D "No I'm fine, I don't want anything, where's it from? Where did you get your sandwich from?"

S "Tesco Express"

D "You got it at Tesco Express, that means nothing to me, I shop at Walmart, it doesn't matter"

S "I don't know what Walmart is. Who are you? Who are you please?"

D "It doesn't matter who I am, I'm a very successful business man, and you've probably seen me on TV quite a lot"

S "I haven't, I haven't"

D "Ok, if I offer you a million dollars for your cafe-shoppe-bar, how much? I mean are you willing to take a million dollars for your cafe-shoppe-bar?"

S "It's not for sale"

D "It's not for sale? So you're not accepting a million dollars from me?"

S "Well, I don't know"

D "I can't believe you aren't accepting a million dollars, I can make the place a goldmine, you can work for me, I'll sponsor your videos, I'll sponsor your videos"

S "I'm, I'm, No, no, I don't know, I don't know who you are"

D "You're not going to accept a million dollars?"

S "No, no"

D "This is unbelievable, what I suggest is that you get off my land, Ok? Cause I'm not having this, this is my land, I'm building all these fantastic buildings round here, Ok. So I suggest you get off my land and that'll be fine, otherwise I'll get my security, Ok thank you"

S "I was only eating my fucking prawn sandwich, love you bye... He's coming back, who the fuck is it? Here look he's harassing me. He's obviously some sort of crank, God I feel awful. This is it when you make videos, you get cranks coming up to you, look is he following me? This is it when you make videos, you get cranks coming up to you because they think they know you. Oh my God, I wish it was real, then I could sell my cafe-bar-shoppe. What I'm going to have to do, is I'm going to have to take my stickers off the side, because they're on the side of the door look, down there, and people can see where it is. Frigging crank, who the fucks that? Love you bye"

Stephanie Aird-59.5k views

It's Not Really Theft

"Hello, I love hotels when they have a shower cap, how mint is that? I love it, I don't even need a shower but I'm going to go in with my shower cap on, look its elastic and everything, love it I do, and it's so big it'll keep my eyebrows not wet so they won't wash off. After I've used it, I'm going to dry it and take it home, and these look... (soaps) I'm going to nick the toiletries, love you bye."

Stephanie Aird-58.6k views

Stuck

"Toby, get help, phwoar you stink man, go over there. Hello, now ya's can't say I'm that clumsy cause I haven't been stuck for ages. The cat had picked up something off the floor and I was shaking it to see what it was, and she's gone in her thing, this scratchy post, and I've tried to get her out and I've got my head and shoulders stuck, and I still don't know what the frig she's took. I haven't been stuck in anything for ages, I was doing dead well, I'm just going to have to stay comfy until Ian comes in, don't know what the frig he's going to do though, bless him. I'm as clumsy as anything; I'll probably snap my neck in half. Toby will you go over there man, you stink.

Go over there, go and get your bone. He's due in soon on his bike, I swear to Christ, if he's got another flat tyre and I have to wait ages I will kick him to death. I'm famished and all and thirsty, this might be my last ever video, I might not survive, Toby don't do that on my forehead please. Toby move, Toby don't do that"

Stephanie Aird-1.6k views

Ian Is Doing My Titends In

"Afternoon, I bring to you.... It's getting very, very close to the end for me and Ian, and I'll tell you for why ma'darlings. He's driving me round the bastard bend, he's putting some air in the tyres now...
Fucking Hell, he's got his tongue out like that, he looks like a right dick... You Alright?
You know how we get stock in for the bar? We can't always afford a lot, we can't, and we saved up to get a bottle of Smirnoff to sell. He comes in with the bags and I heard...
 BANG! CRASH! SMASH and "FUCKING HELL" at the top of his voice, and I knew, just knew what he'd smashed.
He had lots of bottles, some of it was just beer, just very cheap... (Ian taps on the car window) PISS OFF YA DAFT BASTARD, some of it was very cheap, but no, he'd smashed the bottle of Smirnoff all over the kitchen floor. I can just see it now, you know what he said? "It wasn't my fault" well if it wasn't your fault, who the fucking hells fault was it?
And he will not be wrong, he will not be wrong. If he leaves the freezer door open which he does regularly "I didn't leave it open" you did Ian you were the only fucker here, you did "I didn't open it, it must have brushed open when I went past it"

I think I'll drive over his fucking head while he's putting air in the tyres, Love you bye. Have a good look at him while his head is still round, it's going to be fucking flat one of these days."

Stephanie Aird-2.1MILLION views

Female Chubby Brown

"Thank You for all the lovely comments, someones commented and said "Has anybody ever told you, you sound like and look like Chubby Brown" I don't mind being as funny as Chubby Brown, I think hes fucking hilarious, I have to look like him, really? Im not going to say the C word, Im not, Im not, never, I'll never say the C word on video. Love you bye..... The Cheeky Cun........"

Stephanie Aird-49k views

Highlighting And Contouring

"Morning, I bring to you... what's this new culture of makeup putting on? What's it called? Contouring and highlighting, what's all that about? Well I've had a go at it anyway, I bought some and I've had a go. Where are you? Oh hello, I'm not too sure about it to be honest, what do you think? I look like the tin man off the Wizard Of bastard Oz.

Why are we all going for this contouring and highlighting thing? Every buggers walking round like a HD TV Screenshot, why? Why are we making our faces look 3D when they are 3D? They're not flat, unless you've been ran over by a steam roller.

The whole point of shading and highlighting is to make a drawing or painting look 3D or real. We are real! It's a weird old world isn't it? Mind you my nose does look a bit skinnier, I might have to work on my eyebrows though, love you bye. Oh I might blacken my neck out, you won't see my turkey chin"

Stephanie Aird-307k views

<u>Highlighting And Contouring (Continued)</u>

"I'll tell you what would be a bloody good idea for highlighting and contouring, you could contour your hips and arse and boobs highlighted, you could like... down your middle on your rib cage put loads of contour so it looks like they're going in and highlight your boobs so it looks like they're sticking out, and contour your arse on the side so it shaves 6 inches off, and you won't have to have plastic surgery and all that shit for the people who do for some reason.
You wouldn't even have to diet, you could eat and drink what you want and always look thin, Oh My God! Love you bye...
Oh I'm so excited, I need a lot of brown contour powder"

Stephanie Aird-10.4k views

Cheeky Biatch Bastard!!!

"Oh my god, WTF... Someone has just commented on MY own wall or page or whatever it's called on a page, and told me NOT to get sassy.
ARE YOU SHITTING ME?
I'll get bloody sassy if I like.
Eee I'm bouncing, well in my head I am, I can't be bothered to get up and literally bounce.
Maybe on Friday night I might though.
So Lady whatever your name is, I do apologise, I forgot it, I'm rubbish with names. So Lady, I'll be sassy if I like, so shit off, get off my bastard page if you don't like my videos, and tell your mate not to call me a biatch, cheeky little mare, love you's bye...
Not you who said I was sassy and the other one who called me a biatch, the rest of you's. Oh while I'm on, at the weekend its Valentine's Day Specials at my Cafe-Bar-Shoppe... 55 Church Street, Hartlepool. Friday, Saturday and Sunday night I've got like really good music and Sunday night I've got live music and Saturday night I've got live music and bottles of bubbly for two for £9.99 and nice food, and it'll be nice and romantic. I have like nice lights on and all that at my Cafe-Bar-Shoppe...

55 Church Street, Hartlepool. Book a table will you? Or just pop along for a couple of drinks and some music, some snacks and a bit of a laugh. Get off, I've just been tagged. Or... if you want a quiet table in the corner, I can light a candle and all of that, it's lovely in there and cosy and that, and you won't get called sassy or a biatch, them 2 ladies aren't coming off my page I don't think, I wouldn't of thought so, love you bye"

Stephanie Aird-165k views

Selling Skunk In The Street?

"Hello, I'm so tired on a Monday. What's this thing, people going round selling animals? This fella, well fella? this lad, come up to me the other day in the street, in the street!! And he looked a bit, I don't know really, incoherent should we say?
And he asked me if I wanted to buy some skunk. Well firstly it's either a skunk or some skunks, so his English was pretty rubbish anyway.
Where would I keep a skunk? I don't even know what they eat. The frigging house would be riddled with fleas, skunk fleas, and there would be skunk shit all over the place. If he was selling a hamster I would have had it, I do like a hamster, and dogs, I like dogs, love you bye...
People shouldn't get pets if they're going to sell them on, and he can't of cared much for the welfare of it if he's just asking random people in the street to sell his skunk to. I feel sorry for it, do you Toby?"

Stephanie Aird-251k views

A Rock Chicks Phannies

"Hello, it's me again. I've remembered what I was going to tell you now. Last night in the Cafe-Bar-Shoppe, 55 Church Street, Hartlepool, 3 lovely girls came in, well a girl and 2 women, and they were Phannies. There was Sharon, her mam was called Selina and her aunty was called Donna, and Sharon said she was my number 1 fan, how cool is that? She loves me... ME! I was over the moon. Well, oh Phannies is just the end of my name you know Ste-PHANNIE, well because they're fans, they're Phannies, I just thought it was a good name, Phannies. Anyway they come in and we had a chat and a drink, or 4, and do you know what Sharon bought? She bought, you know how I make bags? Well I don't make the bags, I buy the bags, but I decorate them, called 'Styled By Stephanie' designs, and I do them up nice. Well she bought a bag with 'Stephanie on, but she also bought THAT T-shirt, do you know the one I mean? The one that got me into trouble off the authorities 'I did it doggy style at Stephanie's Cafe-Bar-Shoppe, 55 Church Street, Hartlepool on the back. Remember I got it done off me mate at Diva Tees, T-Shirts, I hope I've got the name right. Well that was the one that was hung up on the wall when the authorities came and they went off it.

'I did it doggy style at Stephanie's'It actually means Doggy Style hot dogs, it doesn't mean we get on all fours and that on the cafe floor and hump until the cows come home, if people think we're doing that, then honey bairn........ NO!

Not with my back anyway, anyway she bought that and a bag and she put it on, the T-Shirt, how cool is that? Thank you for coming in my Number 1 Phannie, and the other 2 Phannies, and I saw some other Phannies when I went down the town earlier shopping.

Oh... do you go shopping with your fella? Don't they get on your fucking nerves? Everything I look at in a shop 'Do you need another one of those? Can we afford one of those?' Everything I was looking at, because I was looking at these pleather trousers, you know because I am a rock chick now? Because I write my own songs and sing my own songs, so obviously I'm a rock chick, so I need some. When I told my teenage daughter I got pleather trousers, her eyes went this big, she went 'Mother you better not have' she's just got over the hair, and now I'm going to be wearing pleather trousers. Anyway I got some at peacocks, oh yeah, yeah...

Right back to what I was saying... fellas. Ian is walking around winging about this, that and the other and he's got a sore throat, and its killing he can't hardly talk, for someone with a sore throat who can't hardly talk, he can't half fucking talk. I said here, have one of those, I gave him a packet of sweets and I said 'Just suck on one of those, suck on a fisherman's friend will ya' he gets on my bloody nerves he does. Anyway I'm going to go and try my pleathers on again, where the hell are they? I hope I didn't leave them in McDonalds cafe, love you bye...

Was that what I had to tell them? What was it I had to tell them? It was none of that, none of it, none of it, I can't remember, and I'm not even drunk, strange"

Stephanie Aird-1.4k views

UNBELIEVABLE!!

"Evening, long story alert, I know some of you really like a long story, some of you not so much, I'll have to get my foundation to put my face on for tonight.

Do you know when you're in a relationship girls? And someone says something nice to you or tries to kiss you or something who's not your boyfriend, but you can't help telling your boyfriend because you want him to think your undesirable to everybody else, you know what I'm talking about, you do.

Well someone tried to kiss me yesterday in the Cafe-Bar-Shoppe, 55 Church Street, Hartlepool, so I told Ian, I couldn't help it, so I went 'Ian' he went 'Yes' I said 'Last night at the Cafe-Bar-Shoppe, 55 Church Street, Hartlepool, somebody tried to snog me' he went 'What for?' I said 'Sorry? What for?' I said 'Oh thanks a lot, yeah what for' not 'who was it I'll kill them' or 'Well of course they would, you're completely and utterly delightfully gorgeous ma'darling' no he didn't say none of that he went 'What for?' Heartbroken I was, I said to him 'Well at least one thing you've got sorted' he said 'What?' I said 'The poem that you can put in my Valentine's Day card'

Roses are red, Violets are blue, Why the fuck would anyone want to snog you?

The bastard, love you bye"

Stephanie Aird-27.3k views

Sundays With Ian

"Hello, it's me Stephanie, I bring to you... an update really. Last night was really good at the Cafe-Bar-Shoppe, 55 Church Street, Hartlepool, we had quite a few in, we had a group from Sunderland, Sharon and the crew, they were canny but one of them, Diane, I gave them some cakes and that, she ate the fucking cake wrapper. We had some other lovely people in, there was Hannah, Sam and Lindsay all absolutely gorgeous people and I did a show, like jokes and singing and that, that was good but my throat was really bad so that wasn't good. Anyway we've just been to The Swan to get my tickets to give out and then we've been to the kings arms for our dinner, I couldn't eat all of mine, so I've put some beef in my bag for the dogs, it's made my bag smell a bit better because it smelled foisty because I had it in the loft for a few years and we've took them all out as you know and it just smelled all foisty. Well while we were in there Ian was fucking about with my phone, pissing about with his mate Mick, sending daft texts to each other. I said 'We need to know where the Norton gig is' because I need to know how to get there, he said 'Oh it's alright, we'll go on the way back from here' I said 'Oh that's good' he said 'I know where it is' I says 'Oh that's good' he was pissing about, , and then as we came out to get in the car, he's sat there fannying on so I said 'What are you doing?' he said 'Well I don't know the postcode for the Norton Village thing, I'll have to try and find it on the SatNav' So I said 'Why didn't you do that instead of pissing about with daft texts?' we're still sat here and we will still be sat here in another 20 minutes while he looks for a squirrel, have you seen any squirrels Ian? I'll just sit waiting all my life WAIT, WAIT, WAIT, have you seen a squirrel? Eee I just love Sundays with Ian... Not, let's get home and give the beef to the dogs"

Stephanie Aird-40.3k views

Petrol Station Weekly Excitement

"Hello, I bring to you... The weekly petrol station visit. This is how sad we are, this is our highlight of the week, going to the petrol station, it's the only place we go, and Church Street, what the fuck? We've just pulled up and Ian goes 'I'll put some petrol in have you got any moolah' I goes 'nah' I said 'Use the card' he said 'Is there any money on the card?' I says 'How the fuck do I know?'
You just put the petrol in and try the card don't you? If there's no money on the card they can't take the petrol back out can they? So we're sat there and he always goes like, you know when Gorillas groom each other?
He's always picking at me and plucking my fucking chin, I said 'Are you putting some petrol in or what?' do you know, I'm going to start going somewhere else on a Sunday, I really, really am....
Here he is, here he is, fucking Michael Barrymore on Acid, daft fucker, yeah you, love you bye... Are you done? And stop plucking my fucking chin! Fucking daft twat!"

Stephanie Aird-132k views

Dogs!!!

"Hello, I need to share this with somebody so you might as well be the one, Look... Arse cleaning in stereo... two dogs. I don't know whether I'm in need of anger management or I'm hormonal or whatever it is, but the dogs are getting on my fucking titends! Listen to that sound... Look, all they do is shit and piss and lick their own genitalia. Normally it just goes over my head, I'm not bothered, I'm cuddling them and all that, it's just getting on my nerves, and that noise, all of it, and Toby going around sniffing... What the fuck is he sniffing at?!?! Toby what do you keep sniffing at? Lucy... Hello... Hello, is that all you can do, lick, shit, scratch, piss? Sorry had to share. I feel a little bit better now the weight has been lifted off my shoulders, so any dog owners out there, as much as we absolutely adore our dogs, the question now is, do they get on your nipple titting ends at times? Love you bye... Is it off? Oh and do you have to shake and all? So your frigging whatever goes everywhere, Like everywhere, like every time I sit down to eat you shake and it goes all over my tea, and the sneezing on my foot, day in, day out.

Well there's where they pissed on the fucking floor. I've got two choices, I can either take up Yoga or kill the dogs. Yoga it is, I know I'll end up putting my bastard back out doing that and all"

Stephanie Aird-575 Views

When Fern interviewed Me

An interview with SteFernie...(The freak duo)

Fern: Hi, My names Fern Duggan and today I have a very, VERY, very special guest. Her name...Stephanie Aird. (Applause). We all know and love her from Facebook, YouTube, Instagram, what have you – all the social medias we know her on. Now, Stephanie, thank you for coming on my show.

Stephanie: (Brushing teeth) Aye, it's alright. Thank you for having me.

Fern: You're more than welcome. Now, my first question...our first question; when were you born and where?

Stephanie: Yeah, good question. I was born in 1968 on the 4th of October in London, Lambeth in London. So basically (Singing) 'Maybe it's because I'm a Londoner, that I love London town...Yeaaah'. Next question ma darling?

Fern: Interesting...interesting...what did you want to be when you were younger?

Stephanie: What did I want to be when I was younger? A lot of the time I wanted to be a teacher... and a lot of the time I wanted to be a pop star. It's weird isn't it because I used to be a teacher and now I'm a popstar. (Pauses) Well...nearly a popstar. So$_{34}$ yeah.

Fern: What did you study at Uni? Where did you study at Uni?

Stephanie: I studied at the university of Northumbria and I studied...I did a BA honours with QTS (that's qualified teaching status). Look what I found when I was clearing out my bedroom (Shows us a picture of her when she was graduating).

Fern: What was your favourite thing about being a teacher? I know you were one for a very long time, nearly TWO DECADES!

Stephanie: I had quite a lot of favourite things as a teacher, obviously the students and the banter with the kids. Oh and the school holidays (clicks teeth). Also buying lots of stationary and the challenge and making a difference and all that.

Fern: What's your favourite memory with Ian?

Stephanie: My favourite memory with Ian, ahh the Friday nights. We had Kylie Minogue playing and we would be completely rat-arsed and then we would get a bit...you know...kissy kissy. (Pauses, reminiscing)

....

....

Fern: What annoys you the most?

Stephanie: What annoys me the most is people coming to me with problems instead of solutions. Like Ian, "I can't find my spanner" well don't tell me that!! **(Lamp explodes in bedroom) Oh, and lamps from Argoss, setting fire to my fucking walls. Talking of problems, couldn't of timed that any fucking better. Do I touch it or what?**

Fern: What do you get from McDonalds?

Stephanie: On the rare occasion I go to Maccydees, I get a diet coke or a cappuccino. But if I do get something to eat it is a cheeseburger happy meal.

Fern: What made you want to start making videos?

Stephanie: To be honest, I'm not quite sure. It just sort of happened in the summer holidays of 2014, I mean before that I did a couple, like a few years ago. Then I just started making them...and I couldn't stop. I've gotten myself into a lot of pickles with them, I really, really have.

Fern: Did you ever think you would get famous from it?

Stephanie: At first I didn't, I thought no way, will these make me famous! In fact, I didn't even think about that. But now I know, just gonna happen. I mean, come on! If that doesn't, me singing will. (Pauses) God, I'm starving! I'll tell you what wont make me famous...this fucking fringe.

Fern: What did you want to come out of it? Money? Fame? Tours? Admiration?

Stephanie: Well, I like to entertain people whether its comedy or singing. I like doing gigs and shows! Obviously I like to make records but I do that anyway... In me café-bar-shoppe. 55 CHRUCH STREET, HARTLEPOOL.

Fern: Have you fed the dogs today? That is a very serious question, poor Lucy and Toby. I hope you have fed them.

Stephanie: Eeeeee (Burps) pardon. I don't know. (to dogs) Toby? Lucy? Have I fed ya's today? What day is it? Yeah, I would have, they look ok to me!

Fern: Our final question is…can you ride a unicycle?

Stephanie: (Jumping on trampoline) Can I ride a UNICYCLE?? 'Fuck you on about? 'fucks a unicycle? Like a bike you ride at college? Nah, I can't!

Fern: I didn't think so…

Stephanie: Right, thank you Fern, thanks. Can I go now? You wouldn't believe what's just happened. I'm going to have to go.

Fern: Well Stephanie, it's be a joy having you on our show…my show…the Fernews show. It's the Fern interview show, I am like Piers Morgan except I'm a female and younger…and at university. Tune in next time, where we will be asking YOU for your questions (pause) at some point…when Stephanie has time and I can edit!

Erm…bye.

Oh while I think on..............

In the new chat show me and Al Devon are starting in 2017 in my cafe-bar-shoppe, 55 Church Street, Hartlepool.........
I'm going to be having an "Ask Ya' Aunty Steph" Slot where You can send in emails like a problem/advice page thingy. If you would like to be part of it or if you have something you would like me to help with (well i'll certainly try and help ma' darlings) then email me and please type in the subject line...
ASK YA' AUNTY STEPH, cheers.

stephanieaird1968@gmail.com

Oh and also look out for me new website that will be coming in 2017, that will have all the info on about tour dates, cafe-bar events, meets and greets and evrything :)

What Is It With Men And Boobs?

"Hello, are you alright? It's me Steph, I haven't been on for a while, I've been busy. Do you know when you go out with a fella? And you think that they're looking at pictures of ladies boobs? Well I think Ian might be looking at pictures of ladies boobs, I'm going to see if I can catch the bastard in the act, I'll fucking boob him if he is, shhhh, if he's going to look at anyone's boobs it should be mine, mine are a nice pair and I'll tell you what they haven't half grew since I've been having takeaways and Budweiser and Stella and Cava every night, they're fucking huge, when I sit down they rest on my knees, I'm going to have to go on a diet, shhhh.

Yeah, I heard him jump up quick there, you fucking bastard, I'll look through his history on his laptop later, one tit on there and I'll knock his teeth out, love you bye... Ian what were you doing? Doing what? You were just sat doing nothing? Nothing at all?"

Stephanie Aird-2.1k views

A few of My Limericks

Derek had a little lamb, a kipper and a duck,
He invited all his mates for tea and the kipper
ran out of luck,

Derek had a little lamb, a haddock and a pike,
When he fancied fish for tea, He went to the
chippy on his bike,

Derek had a little lamb, it was the spitting pop
of Hitler, By Christ he could play the violin, it
was one hell of a fucking fiddler,

Derek had a little lamb that's wool had started
to unravel, That's because Derek's mam was
the pop of Jimmy Saville,

Derek had a little lamb, a Womble and a sock,
When he was feeling horny, to Wimbledon
Common the Womble did flock,
When the Womble got there, much to his
dismay, There was Derek and his Lamb in a
bush, oooh I say!

Derek had a little lamb, he took it to the club, When it was the lambs round, it wouldn't take the hint, So unfortunately Derek ate its legs with a lot of fucking mint,

Derek now has no pets, and also has no friends, He's off to visit pets at home god knows how that'll end.

4ft 2in Guinea Pigs!
With Ian

(Putting a chimnea together)

I "There we go that's it"

S "20 hours later"

I "It's not 20 hours later"

S "Yeah you weren't up 20 hours ago, in fact you've been up 2 hours. Do you like Facebook? How long do you sit and scroll through it?"

I "I don't know really, not often, not often."

S "Some of the things people put on... It says here 15 years ago someone bought a guinea pig, because I've joined the guinea pig page"

I "As you do"

S "Yeah, and it says 'fifteen years ago I bought a guinea pig and I liked my Guinea Pig and I stroked it every day, as the years went by my Guinea Pig grew bigger' hang on that bits in Chinese that 'My Guinea Pig grew bigger and bigger and it grew so big it is now 4ft 2'

I "PISS OFF! You can't get a 4ft 2 guinea pig"

S "That's what somebody has put"

I "I think they've probably bought a dog and not realised, it's probably a fucking Dalmatian or something"

S "Stop swearing Ian, there's no need for it"

I "Eee I wonder where this goes (holding a piece of metal)"

S "I know a good place where you could shove it. Oh my god, I've just joined the hamster page, it says 'If you have a hamster and it lives with a Guinea Pig, you must beware because the Guinea Pig is bigger than the hamster and if they were to fight, the Guinea Pig could damage the hamster"

I "No shit!

S " 'If you look carefully at their teeth, you will see that Guinea Pigs teeth are bigger than the hamsters, so in a showdown the hamster would not stand a chance, so Guinea Pigs and hamsters must not live together for this reason.'"

I "Are they shitting us? As if we didn't already know that

S "(Laughing)"

I "It's like saying you can't let a Penguin and a Crocodile live together, it's pretty fucking obvious already isn't it?"

S "Stop swearing! (Laughing)"

I "I'm not going to buy a Penguin and a Crocodile and put it in the same tank to see how they get on... (Struggling to put the frigging chimnea together) Right, that gets applied in that lid but I can't see the point in that but that actually slots in down the chimnea"

S "That's, you know when you have pets and animals, it's to stop them falling in on the flame. Do you know like the big bad wolf in the 3 little pigs how it went down the chimney?"
I "Your talking as much shite as them people on the hamster site"
I "Are you sure you didn't write that review?"
S "No"

Stephanie Aird-15k views

Low Fat Egg Sandwich

"Hello, I'm sat in the car park in Hartlepool, I've just been to boots for a low fat sandwich, and I'll tell you for why ma'darlings... It's all very well and good pretending and imagining that you haven't put weight on and that you've lost weight, but I thought you know what? I'm going to put it to the test to see if it's real, so I got weighed... BIG MISTAKE... BIG MISTAKE... I've put half a fucking stone on since Friday, it's only Monday, who knew, who knew there were so many calories in Cava and curry and chips and pizza and Budweiser, half a clem in 72 hours... ARE YOU SHITTING ME?

Hey ho, still look fabulous though, got a new
top out of Matalan half price. Do you know? I
used to be able to get credit all the time, I was
really good with my credit when I was a
teacher, you know on the Never Never?
Well since I've became self-employed at my
Cafe-Bar-Shoppe, 55 Church Street, Hartlepool,
I can't get credit and I need a Mac Book, a Mac
to do my songs on because my laptop is alright
but I want a Mac, I want one, and I was
thinking the only way I might be able to get one
is to go to them Bright house places, but
something like £17,000 over 45 years, for a
computer, fair enough you're only paying 90p a
week but it's like forever, I might have to do it.
I've never been in this situation before.

I rang my sister, I said 'Can you get credit?'
she said 'Can I Fuck' so that was the end of
that, she said 'Welcome to the blacklist'

So now today I've found out that I can't get
credit and I'm fat as fuck, and it's started
pissing down, absolutely pissing down, and this
sandwich is fucking horrible, love you bye"

Stephanie Aird-2.9m views

Time for a
Troll Slaying Break............

Troll Slaying

#1
Troll – Makes me feel sick, any need to eat like that? Actually? Bork
Stephanie – Yes I need to eat like that, I tried it upside down but I couldn't swallow the bread.

#2
Troll – Ya' getting on my tits now, I've asked loads of times for a shout out from the USA.
Stephanie – This video was made 2 years ago, Id need a time machine to shout you out in this.

#3
Troll – Dirty, what a mess.
Stephanie – Nasty what a troll.

#4
Troll – It's rude to talk with your mouth full, seriously that noise is fucking horrendous. You sound like a Foley artist's porn sound effect.
Stephanie – You'd know, bet you and your hand have had hours of fun viewing it.

#5

Troll – You're a funny woman but seriously, is there any need for you to record yourself eating like a fucking animal?

Stephanie – You're a nasty troll, but seriously is there any need to present yourself typing like a fucking cunt?

#6

Troll – Does the mouth full of food and smacking not bother anyone? Disgusting.

Stephanie – Does the troll full of hate and insults not offend anyone? Cuntish.

#7

Troll – You should have been a stain on a mattress.

Stephanie – No need as I have lots of stains on my mattress, curry, cava, stella and marmalade (dont even ask about the marmalade)

#8

Troll – People like that should be neutered and left in a dark room.

Stephanie – Trolls like you should be de-thumbed and left in Aldi car park.

#9

Troll – Shut your mouth and stop talking when youre eating you fucking slob bitch. I would have been entertained if it wasnt for the chicken mayonnaise and brown bread stuck between your teeth.

Stephanie – Actually it was EGG mayonnaise, even my neighbours hamster new that.

Phannie – Dont look then L**a ya daft trollop.

Troll – Ro***ne with a name that sounds like a Russian alley rat prostitute, pipe down a bit.

Troll – And Stephanie brilliant, that made the world of difference to me, knowing that in fact it was deceased poultry that was hanging round your gums for all to witness and not chicken period.

Stephanie – Ro***ne, I love your name, its not common like some.

Stephanie – L**a for Gods sake it was EGG NOT CHICKEN, how many times ya dozy cunt!!!

#10

Troll – Did your mother ever teach to you never to talk with your mouth full. It sounds like a washing machine on spin cycle lol

Stephanie – No my mother was too busy bitch slapping your mother!!

#11
Troll – Chewing with her gob open makes me feel sick.
Stephanie – Sick bag? 5p please!

#12
Troll – Cant even watch this after listening to about 10 seconds of her chewing dirty.
Stephanie – No, no, the sandwich was clean, very clean indeed AND in date.

#13
Troll – Omg the way she eats. Just want to knock her out.
Stephanie – Id like to see you try ma' darling!!!

#14
Troll – Dye your fookin eyebrows will ya.
Stephanie – DIY ya dick instead of trolling will ya.

#15
Troll – At least finish what you're eating before speaking you clatty cow.
Stephanie – At least troll with some hardcore language you fucking cock.

I am priveleged to say that I have had 1000s of fabulous reviews, thank you so much for taking the time to write such lovely words, here are just a handful and I will gladly print some in every book I write.........................

Mim West reviewed Stephanie Aird –
8 December at 10:39
Fantastic woman. Took the time to out to email me while I've been having a bad ms relapse. Deserves all this success and all the great things in life. I really hope you become massive and have ur own show. We need more hilarious women in the world. Steph aird proper legend. Thank you lovely xxxx

Mark Hague reviewed Stephanie Aird –
5 star
18 December at 10:23 ·
I need to visit stephanies cafe bar shoppe!! Randomly came across your car video last night and never stopped laughing then spent the next 4 hours watching loads you are amazing! Fave laugh out loud one arse is sticky not with shitty vid!! Hahaha come to leeds!! Xxx

Steve Riley reviewed Stephanie Aird –
5 star
2 December at 22:56 ·
Watching all your videos makes me laugh so hard and reminds me to smile even when it's rough! Any plans for you to have tour dates on the south coast yet?

Martyn Sams reviewed Stephanie Aird –
5 star
4 December at 17:33 ·

Top lady Great show on Friday u put on and
best off luck with the rest off your tour dates I
dare say will come and see u again

Donna Hayes reviewed Stephanie Aird –
5 star
4 December at 19:00 ·

I saw one of your videos for the first time
tonight , youre fabulous, too funny with the
control pants! Im howling. You tell it like it is
with style

Stuart Leighton reviewed Stephanie Aird –
5 star
15 December at 16:45 ·

Never heard of Steph before but I'm sat here
laughing to myself and as a long term DJ
entertainer of 35 years I can spot talent and
she's naturally funny must try to go to a show
and heckle her bet I get put right in my place
lol

Heidi Crawford reviewed Stephanie Aird –
5 star
19 December at 18:48 ·
She is bright spontaneous , loves life , and hilarious as hell to watch , makes my day all the way from Australia... with her "I bring to you"

Eric Norton reviewed Stephanie Aird –
5 star
13 December at 04:44 ·
write a revue ? are you taking the piss ? this woman has more talent than anyone , i really hope one day i get to see a live performance, super cool super funny and super talented xxx

Rory Clucas reviewed Stephanie Aird –
5 star
3 December at 11:04 ·
Had a great night last night at the swan. Stephanie made me piss myself laughing. Very talented lady who will go far!

Kirsty Schlechter Payne reviewed Stephanie Aird –
5 star
23 December at 12:18 ·
Omg I absolutely love Stephanie, without fail she makes me giggle in every video, probably the only one I watch every video of and makes me laugh every time.

Julie Curran reviewed Stephanie Aird —
5 star
4 December at 14:34 ·
Stephanie Airds first ever show at the Swan at
Billingham she played to a full house really
enjoyed it she was really funny we would
definitely recommend everyone to go and see
her xx

Rochelle Williamson reviewed Stephanie Aird —
5 star
11 December at 23:04 ·
Not many people make me laugh out loud
except stephanie she is real life one of a few
who is naturally funny she needs her own tv
show

Clare Wooley reviewed Stephanie Aird —
5 star
28 November ·
She is brilliant could watch her all day makes
me laff so much, she is so down to earth too
which makes it even better xx

Connor Gray reviewed Stephanie Aird —
5 star
12 December at 00:15 ·
This woman! Is incredible! Such a genuinely
funny lady! Hilariously and an absolute
genius!! I will 100% be making a trip to
Hartlepool! Feel like I've known her for years!

Kelly Wills reviewed Stephanie Aird —
5 star
9 December at 10:37 ·
I'm wanting a night out in you're pub.
Could u send me the full address please. We all
think your fantastic xx

I'ts 55 Church Street, Hartlepool, Ma' Darling
x

Gill Mills reviewed Stephanie Aird —
5 star
2 December at 08:15 ·
Love her really makes me laugh cheers me up
everytime I watch her she should be on
prescription better than any happy pill. Xxx

Zach Cody Vasquez reviewed Stephanie Aird —
5 star
18 December at 18:56 ·
Down to earth and tells it like it is and if you
can't handle that well.....piss off!

Rachael Childs reviewed Stephanie Aird —
5 star
10 December at 23:42 ·
Cheers me up. Even the f in and jefin just fits
in so perfectly. Cava ,pants and and Ian
brilliant!

Seaneen Corbett reviewed Stephanie Aird –
5 star
15 December at 10:36 ·
Love this girl, relates to so many of us girls
keep it up, u always make me laugh

Mark Hardy reviewed Stephanie Aird –
5 star
15 December at 14:44 ·
This woman is crazy love her videos. Always
makes me laugh when I'm in a foul mood. Keep
up the good work.

Carol Fairclough-bowen reviewed Stephanie
Aird –
5 star
24 December at 10:26 ·
Love love love my calendar signed as requested
too thankyou very much Stephanie xx

Nicole Louise Wotherspoon reviewed Stephanie
Aird –
5 star
11 December at 23:42 ·
Never fails to make me giggle fucking love this
womans videos

Question Time........

My Very helpful Mini-PA, Callum Nicholson, I have mentioned him a lot in my videos, bless him he's only 14 and he is amazing, he has helped with this book and transcribed most of my videos for me, thanks chuck. He is my ghostwriter I shall call him Casper. He asked if he could interview me in the book, yeah wellaye........

An Interview With Stephanie Aird

Q. How Does It Feel To Have Had 2 Sold Out Dates On Your First Ever Tour?
A. It feels unreal, like totally unreal, I keep thinking it was a fluke and worrying that it won't happen again, but then I get excited that it probably will.

Q. What Do You Want To Achieve In The Upcoming Years?
A. I would love to achieve many things, my main thing would be to be able to get through each day without bloody vertigo and anxiety as it hampers too much of what I want to do. If and when my illness goes the sky is the limit to do amazing things for myself, my friends, family and to support other people and somehow reach out to all the souls who email me about going through a hard time.

Q. Are You Planning On Releasing More Music Next Year?
A. Yes, hell yes, totally yes, I can't help it.

Q. Who Would You Most Like To Do A Musical Duet With?

A. Oh God so many, but If I really could it would be my Granda, Dougie Mack (Douglas Macklam), he was a singer did a mean Al Jolson impersonation, and one of my main inspirations, he not here anymore though.

Q. Where Are You Planning On Going On Tour Next Year?
A. 2017 will be Great Britain, Starting off in the North East and aiming further each month.

Q. How Does It Feel To Have Achieved Your Childhood Dream And Get The Fame You Deserve?
A. I don't feel I have yet.

Q. When And Where Did You And Ian First Meet?
A. We met on Facebook as our mutual friend Joanne Boyle introduced us.

Q. If You Could Choose To Be In Any Movie Or TV Show What Would It Be?
A. Ooh fab question... I'm quite a contrary cun... soul I love horror and comedy and all sorts... I'd love to be in Hellraiser, Beauty and the beast and only fools and horses

A big thank you to Stephanie Aird for allowing me to interview her.

Awww and Look, Callum wrote me
this.......
And its all true Ma'Darlings, Yaaaaay.

Stephanie Aird Success Page

125,000 Facebook Page Likes,

130,000 fans on Reverbnation

Over 20 Million Video Views,

5,000 YouTube Subscribers,

1,000 Twitter Followers,

25 BBC Introducing Song Plays

Asked to be in the new Sitcom 'Extra
Extra',

2 Sell Out UK Tour Dates.

and a shot of Aloe Vera for me Tea
(sorry I added that bit)

Before I started making comedy videos I regulary wrote statuses on my Facebook profile. I enjoy making my frinds and family laugh, I was the same at school when I was a kid I was the class clown. And always in trouble for pissing about.

Here is an insight into what my thumbs were upto a few years before they started pressing Record on my phone video..........

Saturday, 15 November 2014 at 23:13 UTC
Stephanie Aird updated her status.
Has opened at least 26 bottles of lager and keeps putting them down somewhere - can't remember drinking them so have I or not? :)

Tuesday, 4 November 2014 at 14:58 UTC
Stephanie Aird updated her status.
Right am done with shameless advertising for the day, I'm off to swill the paths, bath the pup and feather me Pocahontas outfit x

Thursday, 30 October 2014 at 15:50 UTC
Stephanie Aird updated her status.
A man in California in boxed me and called me an ugly retard. Yaaaaaaaaay my videos have reached America :) :) :)

Monday, 20 October 2014 at 17:23 UTC+01
Stephanie Aird updated her status.
FYI i've unlocked all of the previous unavailable videos on my you tube channel, they were locked cos some have foul language in (well they have the odd 'shite' in) well now I'm not a public servant :) I can have them safely available for your viewing pleasure lol, theres 219 in all, Jesus I've been one busy crazy lady xxx

Stephanie Aird shared a video: Movie on 08-12-2011 at 10.17.
The first videos I ever made on fb were in 2011, no bugger batted an eye lid then all of a sudden in August 2014 the shit hit the fan at full speed lol x

Stephanie Aird updated her status.
Thanks so much for all the lovely comments and in-box messages. I have had many questions mainly asking if I left my job because of my comedy videos and the kerfuffle they caused. I have the kerfuffle from my comedy videos to thank whole heartedly for giving me the kick up the backside I needed to make a change to my life. After a lot of illness, some of which was made worse from obvious pressures in a busy job I now have the chance to recuperate and think about my next adventures :) xxx

Stephanie Aird updated her status.
Loving my shiny new life - excited for my new adventures :) I've enjoyed 18 mostly wonderful years as a teacher, I took the brave decision to leave school because I need a new challenge, a different direction and to give birth to many new ventures :) I take with me fond memories of many amazing students and colleagues- happiness and love to you all :) xxx

Thursday, 9 October 2014 at 22:12 UTC+01
Stephanie Aird updated her status.
The best inbox I've read lmfao from anon: he said he was going to come back at ten but tbh I don't think he will. If he does stay out all night again then he'll be sorry cause I'm not putting up with his poop anymore. I AM AN INDEPENDENT WHITE WOMAN WHO DON'T NEED NO MAN

Thursday, 9 October 2014 at 21:09 UTC+01
Stephanie Aird updated her status.
Am high as a kite from practicing I'm gonna go a get a bottle of dandelion and burdock to come down x

Thursday, 9 October 2014 at 18:26 UTC+01
Stephanie Aird updated her status.
There's some cheeky little buggers who want a bloody good hiding, no respect some kids. And I don't blame the parents cos I've met many lovely parents who have dog snot for offspring!!!!

Thursday, 9 October 2014 at 18:34 UTC+01
Stephanie Aird updated her status.
I have calmed the hell down now hahaha I do apologise for my foul language but hey - cussing is such fun ain't it :)

Stephanie Aird updated her status.
Tonight is first attempt at stand up comedy
plus a bolt on of singing/guitar performance :)
here goes something..........

Stephanie Aird updated her status.
Oh bloody brilliant night at the Fishermans
Arms. I totally loved the acts that were on and
especially loved the support I got for my set,
onwards and upwards in my new venture :)

Stephanie Aird updated her status.
To the pile of dog shit threatening and abusing
3 lovely youngsters last night near greyfields -
a passing witness has named one of ya' now
I'm going to the police to shame ya'.

Stephanie Aird updated her status.
I do apologise for my previous anger filled
status, I will re write it now i'm calm. To the
large GANG of bullies who picked on 3 pacifist
youngsters last night near greyfields - your
behaviour will not be tolerated by decent living
people and I now have 4 names to hand in to
police.

Friday, 9 March 2012 at 20:59 UTC
Stephanie Aird updated her status.
I reckon it should be legal to crack someone
over the head with a whisky bottle after they
violently rape ya. I also reckon it should be
four for a fiver on stella not just three. Ps im
on about corrie dont worry i havnt turned total
vigilante.

Saturday, 17 March 2012 at 08:28 UTC
Stephanie Aird updated her status.
Everywhere is made toddler proof, gate on,
high chair up, toys out, ornaments away,
anything mouth size hidden, dog in dog house,
cat cautioned, sprays bleaches and liquids
banished. All sharp corners on every glass
table covered. All remotes put up high. All
floors hoovered low. Plugs wires and electricals
made safe. Doors locked. Quavers open Taps off
tight. Biscuit lid loose. Cot up. Radiators turned
down. Right I think that's it. Jeeeesus. And I
thought it took a long time to plan lessons for
multpile classes of thirty pupils. :Saturday, 17
March 2012 at 21:01 UTC
Stephanie Aird updated her status.
I swear (yes I know I do regularly) to God I
have theee best behaved and most gorgeous
grandson EVER. I have though i cant help
saying it, what a little angel he is :) (don't
worry girls I know you GILFS Out there are like
me, you think yours are the best but really
mine is

Saturday, 24 March 2012 at 08:09 UTC
Stephanie Aird updated her status.
I've got a feeling, it's familiar I know I have
had it before, I can't quite put my finger on it,
let me think............ahh yes that's it THE FCN
HANGOVER FROM HELL.

Saturday, 24 March 2012 at 08:37 UTC
Stephanie Aird updated her status.
Yay I'm up and about. I laugh in your face
hangover. 8 little stubbies kick the arse out of
8 big Stella's :) I now know the way forward.
At last I have found the meaning of life. Get
pissed on a Friday just stop drinking while still
conscious.

Saturday, 24 March 2012 at 10:24 UTC
Stephanie Aird updated her status.
Oooh this is the life, day off, teen out with
mates, dog in the garden, cat asleep (or dead
not sure which) me lovely fella at work earning
extra pennies for me lovely lager. Think I'll lay
in bed and watch tv quietly, eating sweets and
crisps and drinking fizzy pop just cos I CAN .
Saturday, 24 March 2012 at 10:54 UTC
Stephanie Aird updated her status.
Almost choking to death on a chicken crisp, not
a good look. Note to self: snack in bed by all
means, try it sitting up FFS.

Friday, 30 March 2012 at 18:12 UTC+01
Stephanie Aird updated her status.
Not often ya hearing sawing when someone
is putting up a kitchen blind. I daren't go
and look to see what Ian is doing. FFS

Sunday, 1 April 2012 at 09:15 UTC+01
Stephanie Aird updated her status.
Scrabble tiles, lager bottles, green ginger
puddles, poppadoms and pilau rice all over.
Either we've been burgled or me and Ian are
right Saturday night slobs. (God only Knows
what that stain is on the rug).

Wednesday, 4 April 2012 at 20:35 UTC+01
Stephanie Aird updated her status.
Booked our first holiday abroad together me
and Robbo. (If im with me fella i won't be
able to go out on the pull but on the plus side
I won't have to go to the bar either:).

Tuesday, 10 April 2012 at 11:15 UTC+01
Stephanie Aird updated her status.
No need for slimming and excercise. Just go
the dentist, I sat in a comfy chair for ten
minutes and lost 68 pounds :) FFS

Tuesday, 17 April 2012 at 18:56 UTC+01
Stephanie Aird likes Shaving your pet guinea
pig, because you can.

Friday, 13 April 2012 at 23:06 UTC+01
Stephanie Aird updated her status.
It's very rare these days that something totally
pisses me off (either cos I'm older, wiser,
calmer, generally a happy sole or cos am
usually full of Stella) but I have to say this
virgin TiVo box is a load of fcn hyped up total
bollicking bastard shite.

Wednesday, 2 May 2012 at 20:15 UTC+01
Stephanie Aird updated her status.
While I sat on a bench in the town today with
my shopping a very old woman sat down for a
rest and we had a natter and a bit of a laugh.
When she left she said to me "thanks for your
company". Just thought I'd share that thought
provoking occurrence.

Tuesday, 8 May 2012 at 21:32 UTC+01
Stephanie Aird updated her status.
It's well class planning two engagement do's.
one is sweet and quaint for the nearest and
dearest and one is an almighty scribbling piss
up for the nearest, dearest and fcn mental :)
yes I'm only invited to the second.

A BIT OF BREAK COMING UP..............
EITHER PUT THE KETTLE ON OR READ
Secrets, Revelations and Other
TitBits............OoooH

Secrets, Revelations and Other TitBits

Shhhh....
Before I went on Judge Rinder me and the two
Nikki's drag Queens promised we would half
the money of any we received in compensation.
Although it was a real situation (well real-ish)
We are very good friends and I would never sue
them in real life.
In the next book I will reveal who won and how
much compensation was paid. But by then you
May have seen the show as its on next week,
yaaaay can't wait.

Eeeeeek...
I lost my virginity at 13 years old, the lad was
only 14, bless him. It was very awkward and
particualry pleasant, it was either cos we were
to young or maybe he was just shite at it.

OMG.....
I used to smoke joints regularly when I was a
teen, dear God it used to make me ill, but the
crowd I was in with did it, so I did, how totally
stupid is that. These days im a leader not a
followerer, hahaha.

Shhh...

Talking of drugs... Ian has NEVER done anything like that in his entire life. He's never had a cigarette or done ANYTHING wayward as a teen. So I thought that he needed a second blast at youth when he met me................

I found what looked like a piece of dope in my teens room years ago and put it in the cupboard out of harms way. When I remembered it was there one night I talked Ian into eating half of it with me. Jesus he took some persuading, any way I got him pissed and fed him the dope, we both sat there waiting for something to happen. For some reason I asked had he ever wrote his name with a marker outside when he was a teen.

Yet again he hadn't, so.......

I talked him into coming out to write our names on the bus stop with a sharpie, fuck me, he did and all.

Nothing happened with the dope. My daughter has since revealed it wasn't dope, it was a lump of clay/mud, she only had it to look good in front of her friends. Fucking hell.

Tit bits

I make and sell lovely mirrors, CDs, Canvases, Bags and other art and crafts.....I fucking LOVE pissing about with glitter. I also make felt, knitting and weaving with plastics and wool.......Oh and dream senders, I love doing it all. Before I was a music teacher I was an art teacher............you can imagine the mess I got into with glitter, tissue paper, glue and feather with classes of 30 kids. Eeeeee I loved it and yes I do miss it at times but I dont miss the shitty paperwork that ended up taking more time to do and less time spent with the kids......I'm upset now im gonna get me glitter out and make something. See ya later.......

Heres a few more of my status updates for ya' while I realign my Shakra................

Friday, 19 August 2011 at 16:15 UTC+01
Stephanie Aird updated her status.
bloody boiling :)

Wednesday, 17 August 2011 at 23:18 UTC+01
Stephanie Aird updated her status.
as if i me bikini bottom is floating off on a lilo,
i hope with all me might that ive got a skirt on,
am a f@ck looking down. Oooh i can see the pub
from here :)

Wednesday, 17 August 2011 at 18:08 UTC+01
Stephanie Aird updated her status.
as if sir alan sugar is laid on a sun lounger,
sipping fanta orange in a pair of primark
swimming trunks.

Wednesday, 17 August 2011 at 18:03 UTC+01
Stephanie Aird updated her status.
has the same initials as stella artois how cooool
is that. Cooler than me, its fcn mafting hot here
:). Think ill down a barrel of S.A.

Stephanie Aird updated her status.
ahh, i shall take with me all the wonderful
memories of ibiza, bluest of skies, softest of
sand, the gentle waves on the sea, me sipping
my seventh stella whilst in the background, the
nightly chorus of Oi missus we know its a
topless resort but FFS put ya tits away the kids
are trying to eat their nuggets and chips.

Stephanie Aird updated her status.
well ibiza can heave a big sigh of relief, we've
landed in newcastle. Pub.

Stephanie Aird updated her status.
you can reach me by railway, you can reach
me by trailway, you can reach me with an air
balloon, you reach me with your mind. You can
reach me by caravan, across the dessert like
an arab man, you can reach me anyway except
by bastard text in spain.

Stephanie Aird updated her status.
even i, yes ME of all people is sick of drinking,
i dont think i can face another fcn stella
tonight. Im going to have to be very selfless
and take one (possibly eight) for the team.
Team pissheads, onwards and downwards.

Friday, 26 August 2011 at 16:09 UTC+01
Stephanie Aird updated her status.
by christ! Them wibbley, wobbley trevorboards
are bloody brilliant. Lost 2lb since tuesday.
Who would have thunk that just standing for
10 minutes a day shaking like kerry catona in
an iceland advert could help ya lose weight.
Each new day amazes the shit out of me.

Saturday, 3 September 2011 at 19:04 UTC+01
Stephanie Aird updated her status.
how magical and awesome are dolphins. No im
not pissed yet.

Friday, 23 September 2011 at 16:57 UTC+01
Stephanie Aird updated her status.
note to self: dont fiddle around in ya handbag
to look for jelly babies while drivin', a glycerin
suppositry popped in ya mouth gives ya one
hell of a shock
 especially when doin an illegal u turn to catch
poundstretcher before it shuts. Still amazes me
that i can get a weeks shoppin for £9.20. And
me suppositry lasted all the way through me
shoppin, a jelly baby wouldnt have.

Friday, 23 September 2011 at 17:20 UTC+01
Stephanie Aird updated her status.
back by popular demand: "guess who i just
seen at tesco express". Shirl from eastenders
buying mr kiplings almond slices, i kid you not,
and she got into a white k reg fiat panda.

Stephanie Aird updated her status.
strange conicidences keep happening, usually
on a weekend aswell to add to the strangeness.
I get pissed right, then the next morning the
hangover from fcn hell appears, EVERY TIME,
twilight zone or what

Stephanie Aird updated her status.
sends a postcard from abroad. Woke with the
hangover from hell after an extremely late
night watching 2 women dress as mary poppins
drinking gin and lady gaga covered in black
balloons. Today ive bobbed in the sea, nearly
puked in the sea asked my neice not to piss in
the sea and saved the teen from nearly
drowning in the fcn sea. Bought chips for the
teen, chips with gravy for the teen and 6 ice
fcn creams for me mam, neice and 2 which
were dropped by the teen. Watched a green
parrot ride a...

Stephanie Aird updated her status.
is lovin' ibiza :) the teen is turning some heads
like with her turquoise hair or is it me, its a
topless beach but ive gone bottomless, not
getting my tits out for no one.

Friday, 29 July 2011 at 15:42 UTC+01
Stephanie Aird updated her status.
as if a seagul is sitting on the roof of me car in
the car park. If its looking for food from me i
hope it likes tins of tomatoes from
poundstretcher.
Friday, 29 July 2011 at 13:06 UTC+01
Stephanie Aird updated her status.
is taking her grandson to the shows :). I'll
chuck him on the tea cups, pay for 10 rides
and sit in his buggy drinking stella. Friday
afternoon, sorted :)

Friday, 29 July 2011 at 12:59 UTC+01
Stephanie Aird updated her status.
flog the horse no longer, the poor thing lives no
more.

Friday, 29 July 2011 at 11:08 UTC+01
Stephanie Aird updated her status.
curried spinach for breakfast, fiery is as fiery
does :)

Thursday, 28 July 2011 at 20:02 UTC+01
Stephanie Aird updated her status.
as if my grandson has learned to open drawers
and put things in. Can i bollox find the remote
control or the bottle opener.
Wednesday, 27 July 2011 at 18:00 UTC+01
Stephanie Aird updated her status.
well here goes, watch out for me on look north,
im the one in full riot gear with gucci bag and
heels.

Stephanie Aird updated her status.
could very easily eat, 6 richmond sausages,
fish, chips, chicken jalfezi, nan, spring roll,
chips, chees burger, chips and a bag of chips.
However, one wants to look good on hols in a
bikini (yes even grannies can wear fcn bikinis)
so...... Tin of tomatoes from poundstretcher it
is then, did i mention what bargains there are
in poundstretcher. 25p for a tin of toms AND
they were new, none of this "used', "nearly...

Stephanie Aird updated her status.
shopping done (fcn baragin at that), cook tea
(using afore mentioned bargains), then off to
the march to try to save the hospital. Come on
now you lot, join in, just an hour of ya time, its
important. 7pm at the library ramp :)

Stephanie Aird updated her status.
OMG, like O M G, as if ive just nipped to
poundstretcher for some bin bags and ended up
getting a weeks shopping in for £18.65, OOO
MMM GGG, it really does stretch ya pounds. I
swear i have never seen a 2ltr bottle of soy
sauce before, its huge and only 99p its like
being back in the 80s yet again :)

Sunday, 24 July 2011 at 11:11 UTC+01
Stephanie Aird updated her status.
F@CK IN HELL, i have definately fell out with
that twat stella.

Saturday, 23 July 2011 at 18:34 UTC+01
Stephanie Aird updated her status.
tragic about Amy Winehouse, loved her brilliant
music that accompanied many fabulous party
nights and brightened up many lonely nights.
RIP.

Wednesday, 20 July 2011 at 19:15 UTC+01
Stephanie Aird updated her status.
might not get there tonight (feel like shite), if i
dont perk up, have a brill night, see ya soon
dykie crew xxx

Wednesday, 20 July 2011 at 15:37 UTC+01
Stephanie Aird updated her status.
come on now, you know what's out,
schoooooooools out :)

Tuesday, 19 July 2011 at 20:43 UTC+01
Stephanie Aird updated her status.
as if one of me friends just had to rake £1.60
together out the copper jar for a bottle of stella.
Phew, thank Christ i had just enough with 2
pence left over. I mean at least she did.

Stephanie Aird updated her status.
aren't fellas brill yet bastard hopeless at the
same time. My lovely yet hopeless fella kindly
yet uselessly did my garden yesterday, did a
stirling yet shite job as he made the garden
look lovely whilst running the mower over the
strimmer he left lying around (how the f@ck he
couldnt see is beyond the realms of reality)
thus slicing the whole cable to shreds and
rendering it fcn usueless, so for doing the
garden...

Stephanie Aird updated her status.
come on, tell the truth, whos shitified by the
lightening and grumbling thunder, i know me
dog is a bit flummoxed, she keeps half barking
then shutting up when it flashes again, the
pussy. ME, am not scared at all......ive got Julie
Andrews to sit on the bed and sing with......

Rain drops on roses and shit on your kittens,
stella thats so cold that you have to wear
mittens. Brown paper phone bills and gas thats
sky high, these are the days when i think.....oh
fuck why.

Stephanie Aird updated her status.
just like a baby, ive had me bath, bottle and
now bed :) well ive had me bottle anyway.

Stephanie Aird updated her status.
jeeeeeeesus how fcn heavy are the soaps, i
watch them for a bit of escapism and yet i find
meself polishing me noose with every episode!
FFS

Stephanie Aird likes Sleep.

Stephanie Aird updated her status.
Note to self (ref: teen being a twat): next time
you change your home phone provider,
remember to reinstate mobile phone barring,
FFS!

Stephanie Aird updated her status.
spending time with my blue eyed, blonde curly
haired, smiling grandson is uplifting, soul
fulfilling and PRICELESS. Spending time with
my mascara strewn black eyed, purple/pink
haired, face like a wet monday morning in
goole, teenager.......nice-less!

Stephanie Aird updated her status.
thank f@ck for that, here she is........yoohoooo
stella, come to mama.

Stephanie Aird updated her status.
eeee i cant believe how good my teen is. Good
at dissapearing, should have called her debbie
maggee only not so fcn lovely :)

Stephanie Aird updated her status.
monday night is the new monday
morning.........fcn teenagers!!!

Stephanie Aird updated her status.
monday morning is the old monday morning.

Stephanie Aird updated her status.
saturday night is the new christmas day :)

Stephanie Aird updated her status.
iiiiaaaaaannnnnnnnn, ya better be reading ya
phone messages, iiiiiaaaannnnnnn x im in real
need of chips! ill make it worth ya while ;) (ill
hold ya hand tonight when im very very drunk,
well maybe ish)

Oh before I forget here's the lyrics to two of my Christmas songs, these went down a treat at my Cafe-Bar Shows in December........

Stephanie's Church Street Wonderland

(to the tune of WinterWonderland)

V: I Bring to you....... are you listening, no funerals but we do Christenings, we're empty tonight, that don't seem right,
 at 55 Church street, Hartlepool

V: Where the fuck are all you punters, I don't care if you are munters,
just get yaselves in, for stella or gin,
 at 55 Church street Hartlepool

C: We can even do you cheesy nachos (nachos) and cover them with tasty garlic sauce.
You might ask me can i do ya' bacon, i'll put on the frying pan of course, course, course.

V: Later on i'll entertain ya, if you're a troll i'll name and shame ya',
 i'll sing ya me songs, i might get them wrong,
at 55 Church street Hartlepool.

C: As the night progresses i'll get pisster, and sing me little heart out just for you.
I get, the occasional cheeky Mister, who calls me a clip, and i will say fuck you, you you.

V: Now me bar..... is full of laughter, some weekends we're packed the rafters, people come far to shoppe-Cafe-Bar,
at 55 church street Hartlepool,
Make—— your—— destination —— Hartlepool!

A fat C*nts Pre-Christmas Carol
(12 days of Slimming)

On the first day of my diet my slimming
brought to me a shot of aloe vera for me tea

On the second day of me diet my slimming
brought to me
2 fibre capsules and a shot of aloe vera for me
tea.

On the 3rd day of me diet my slimming brought
to me
3 slim fast milk shakes, 2 fibre capsules and a
shot of aloe vera for me tea.

On the 4th day of me diet my slimming brought
to me
4 ripe bananas, 3 slim fasts milk shakes, 2
fibre capsules and a shot of aloe vera for me
tea.

On the 5th day of me diet my slimming brought
to me
5 Boring THINGS!!!!!
with 4 ripe bananas, 3 slim fast milk shakes, 2
fibre capsules and a shot of aloe vera for me
tea.

On the 6th day of me diet my slimming
brought to me
6 slices of pizza, 5 Boring THINGS!!!!!
4 ripe bananas, 3 slim fast milk shakes, 2
fibre capsules and a shot of aloe vera for me
tea.

On the 7th day of me diet my slimming
brought to me
7 bottles of stella, 6 slices of pizza, 5 Boring
THINGS!!!!!
4 ripe bananas, 3 slim fast milk shakes, 2
fibre capsules and a shot of aloe vera for me
tea.

On the 8th day of me diet my slimming
brought to me 8 swigs of cava, 7 bottles of
stella, 6 slices of pizza, 5 Boring THINGS!!!!!
4 ripe bananas, 3 slim fast milk shakes, 2
fibre capsules and a shot of aloe vera for me
tea.

On the 9th day of me diet my slimming
brought to me
9 chicken batter ball, 8 swigs of cava, 7 bottles
of stella, 6 slices of pizza, 5 Boring THINGS!!!!!
4 ripe bananas, 3 slim fast milk shakes, 2
fibre capsules and a shot of aloe vera for me
tea.

On the 10th day of me diet my slimming brought to me
a 10 item breakfast, 9 chicken batter ball, 8 swigs of cava, 7 bottles of stella, 6 slices of pizza, 5 Boring THINGS!!!!!
4 ripe bananas, 3 slim fasts milk shakes, 2 fibre capsules and a shot of aloe vera for me tea.

On the 11th day of me diet my slimming brought to me
11 returns to the buffet, a 10 item breakfast, 9 chicken batter ball, 8 swigs of cava, 7 bottles of stella, 6 slices of pizza, 5 Boring THINGS!!!!!
4 ripe bananas, 3 slim fast milk shakes, 2 fibre capsules and a shot of aloe vera for me tea.

On the 12th day of me diet my slimming brought to me
12 fucking pound on!!!
cos of the—11 returns to the buffet, a 10 item breakfast, 9 chicken batter ball, 8 swigs of cava, 7 bottles of stella, 6 slices of pizza, 5 Boring THINGS!!!!!
4 ripe bananas, 3 slim fast milk shakes, 2 fibre capsules and a

MIGHT ASWEL HAVE CHIPPY FOR ME TEA!!!!!!!

After all that I'm going for a lie down in a dark room. I'll be back in an hour............................Have a scroll through some more of me all time fave statuses...........................

Stephanie Aird updated her status.
ian, get me a carton of curry with that fritter
oh and a bag of chips pleeeeaaase x

Stephanie Aird updated her status.
Going to a wedding today, got a lovely new
dress and even a pretty flower for me hair,
shame im shaking like a 90 year old shitting
dog from drinking a keg of LCL.

Stephanie Aird updated her status.
Brilliant night, surreal aint the word, as IF
elvis, marilyn monroe and 5 cowboys were in
the smallies last night :| strange.com. guess
where im going next friday.

Stephanie Aird updated her status.
OMG as IF am in the smallcrafts drinkin' LCL, i
did love 1988, glad to be back again. I SWEAR
its the SAME door, barmaid and bag of scampi
fries.

Stephanie Aird updated her status.
friday night is the new christmas morning :)
Stephanie Aird updated her status.
friday afternoon is the new christmas eve :)

Friday, 1 July 2011 at 11:36 UTC+01
Stephanie Aird and Lesley Smith are now friends.

Friday, 1 July 2011 at 07:55 UTC+01
Stephanie Aird updated her status.
friday is the new friday, 2 fridays in the week, niiiiiice.

Friday, 24 June 2011 at 18:32 UTC+01
Stephanie Aird updated her status.
if theres 1 thing i love its friday, if theres 2 things i love its friday nights and if theres 3 things i love its friday nights with the ones i love.

Friday, 6 May 2011 at 13:15 UTC+01
Stephanie Aird updated her status.
has decided, im out tonight, lock up anything with a pulse.

Friday, 29 April 2011 at 13:53 UTC+01
Stephanie Aird updated her status.
its beautiful and a stunning sight, ive watched in awe and listened attentatively all morning, even shedding a tear when the choir performed Jerusalem but where the f@ck is neighbours, dont push it!

Friday, 17 June 2011 at 14:56 UTC+01
Stephanie Aird updated her status.
oooh ive never ever ever had a tatoo, should i get one??? I really shouldnt be left alone for long periods of time.

Friday, 17 June 2011 at 14:55 UTC+01
Stephanie Aird updated her status.
the c@ sh@ on the m@ the dirty little tw@.

Friday, 17 June 2011 at 13:12 UTC+01
Stephanie Aird updated her status.
what smells of fish and says "heeey". Henry winkle. Well i have to do something on me day off :)

Friday, 17 June 2011 at 13:05 UTC+01
Stephanie Aird updated her status.
i do like fridays me like.

Friday, 27 May 2011 at 20:04 UTC+01
Stephanie Aird updated her status.
pub, home, fridge, kylie, sorted.

Thursday, 16 June 2011 at 21:06 UTC+01
Stephanie Aird updated her status.
ahh there she is.......a vision in red and white, stella, you're so chilled whats your secret. That reminds me, i really should visit the fridge.

Thursday, 16 June 2011 at 21:02 UTC+01
Stephanie Aird updated her status.
is talkin' bollox instead of enjoying having the
house to herself for a b@stard change :) teen at
dads, bloke at work, dog asleep, goldfish dead
(ish), c'mon woman enjoy it.

Thursday, 16 June 2011 at 20:59 UTC+01
Stephanie Aird updated her status.
Hi honey am f@ckin' off to the pub.

Thursday, 16 June 2011 at 20:47 UTC+01
Stephanie Aird updated her status.
hi honey i'm home.

Tuesday, 31 May 2011 at 15:45 UTC+01
Stephanie Aird updated her status.
ooh what shall i have to drink tonight.

Monday, 30 May 2011 at 21:35 UTC+01
Stephanie Aird updated her status.
night 4 on the piss, oh dear, all these school
holidays may just finish me off :). Always
knew i was in the wrong job should have been
pop star, like kylie, only shitter.

Tuesday, 17 May 2011 at 22:06 UTC+01
Stephanie Aird updated her status.
dont get mad, get a plan of action and never
forget the age old tradition and trusted addage,
go fuck yourself!

Sunday, 15 May 2011 at 11:35 UTC+01
Stephanie Aird updated her status. well there it is in a nutshell..........fcn shite.

Sunday, 15 May 2011 at 10:28 UTC+01
Stephanie Aird updated her status.
a whole day and night to do whatever i want, what should i do, the world is my mussel.

Saturday, 14 May 2011 at 22:30 UTC+01
Stephanie Aird updated her status.
teenagers scare the living shit out of me.

Saturday, 14 May 2011 at 21:21 UTC+01
Stephanie Aird updated her status.
jesus some men are fcn pricks. Not jesus ofcourse, he was a nice, kind man apparently.

Saturday, 14 May 2011 at 20:22 UTC+01
Stephanie Aird updated her status.
20 past carling, time flies when ya canning fun.

Monday, 16 May 2011 at 10:37 UTC+01
Stephanie Aird updated her status.
changes come at ya like shit off a stick.

Saturday, 14 May 2011 at 13:51 UTC+01
Stephanie Aird updated her status.
eminen to the 3 degrees, when will i see you again, who the frig is DJing, must be the bloke off the till cos he's shite at picking tunes.

Saturday, 14 May 2011 at 13:43 UTC+01
Stephanie Aird updated her status.
4lb off, back of the net.

Saturday, 14 May 2011 at 13:41 UTC+01
Stephanie Aird updated her status.
wellaye, a radio roadshow on the marina at fcn
comet of all places and as if theyre blasting out
eminem and rhianna and his swear words are
dubbed from f@ckin to chuffing lol.

Friday, 6 May 2011 at 16:06 UTC+01
Stephanie Aird updated her status.
ooh its lovely laying, reading in the
conservatory, i love wickes me. Not sure why
the woman on the till is giving me funny looks
like.

Friday, 6 May 2011 at 14:21 UTC+01
Stephanie Aird updated her status.
any ideas for a DAY out tomorrow? Done
seaton AND tesco bit stumped as where to next
:) (somethin out the ordinary plz.)

Tuesday, 3 May 2011 at 19:31 UTC+01
Stephanie Aird updated her status.
im scared, like really scared. When i was a teen
i absolutely loved barry manilow (well am
sorry and sad but i did), i just watched him on
the one show, i got the shock of me bastard life
and ive had a few shocks, i can tell ya.

Monday, 25 April 2011 at 10:07 UTC+01
Stephanie Aird updated her status.
to quote the words of the famous philosopher,
britney the great, "ooops i did it AGAIN".

Sunday, 24 April 2011 at 17:19 UTC+01
Stephanie Aird updated her status.
has done the family thing all day, MILF and
GILF, its the friends thing tonight STELLA and
FILTH.

Friday, 22 April 2011 at 12:03 UTC+01
Stephanie Aird updated her status.
bacon be got, hangover be gone. Oooh think ill
go out tonight. Robbo get ya purse out :).

Thursday, 21 April 2011 at 15:48 UTC+01
Stephanie Aird updated her status.
theeee perk of working in education ....
H O L I D A Y S ! ! ! Oh and a klix key.

Tuesday, 5 April 2011 at 10:40 UTC+01
Stephanie Aird updated her status.
i wonder if leave my head under my pillow the
dizzy fairy will leave me a pound and take
away my vertigo

Saturday, 2 April 2011 at 17:56 UTC+01
Stephanie Aird updated her status.
men are from mars, well at least some of them
should f@ckoff there.

Ooooh Ive just remembered some more Secrets, Revelations and Other TitBits...............

As a teen my nickname was Doll, becasue I used to wear a lot of make up. On nearly every bench on the Headland I had writtem Doll Loves ******* (I darent put my exes name he might not want it in, imagins the kerfuffle if I got sued, paying a pound a week in compo).

OMG.....
As ya' starting to realise I was a bit of a bastard as a teen.......I used to shoplift records and posters from well known shops. I was really quite good at it, I mean posters are quite long but I managed somehow, to be fair though they didnt have cameras and all that stuff back in them days. I do apologies for nicking and I wont be doing it again.
Got no fucking chance nower days with CCTV every where ya' turn.

OOOh i'm gonna have to do more status updates they do make me laugh, it's weird cos I dont remember writing most of them so its like reading something for the first time.........
It's also quite emotional reading them as a lot are from when I was a teacher and it's brought back so many happy memories...............

Stephanie Aird updated her status.
no work, no exercise, no shopping, no going out
on the piss, vertigo can f@ck right off! The only
thing that ever stopped me doing stuff. On the
brighter side my D. I. V. O. R. C. E. Is ticking
along nicely, s l o w l y, but nicely. It will be
nice to be a "miss" again, albeit a vertigo
ridden, dizzy miss.

Stephanie Aird updated her status.
I wonder how many lives facebook has saved,
cos if there was only the telly and no fb for
entertainment while im ill, I would actually and
literally hang me bastard self! (I have actually
tried but kept falling off the stool due to me
effing vertigo). Oooh, change of plan, not gonna
die just yet, neighbours is on.

Stephanie Aird updated her status.
I am soooo proud of my teen: abbie passed her
grade 1 drumming exam with 88% and
distinctions. I dont usually show off on here
and in fact prefer to share all my mishaps,
alcohol fuelled f@ck ups and naughty
philanderings, but on this occasion.......... GO
ON ABBIE what a STAR *************!!!!!!!!!!!

Wednesday, 9 March 2011 at 18:46 UTC
Stephanie Aird updated her status.
grandsons 1st birthday already, time flies
even faster in GILF mode. Im a proper nana
now like i cant work out how to upload the
photos of his party, ill stick to knitting stella
can cosies.

Friday, 4 March 2011 at 17:56 UTC
Stephanie Aird updated her status.
got weighed today after excercising all week
and living on ryvita and cucumber sprinkles
and had put 5lb on. I will seriously have to
stop wearing these fcn ankle weights cos i
forget i have them on. Me thighs are like
rocks now like.

Wednesday, 2 March 2011 at 18:47 UTC
Stephanie Aird updated her status.
OMJC, just been for a jog with me dog, worked
hard so i though i'd nip in tesco express for a
stella, just the one mind, everyone was
looking at me, even lass stacking cabbages, i
still had me ankle weights on, bright bastard
pink with a "Davina xx" logo sprawled
across, F F S

Monday, 24 January 2011 at 19:49 UTC
Stephanie Aird updated her status.
squeezed in gym after neighbours and before
emmerdale, now thats dedication (not sure
whether im dedicated to the gym or shite tv).

Thursday, 20 January 2011 at 19:31 UTC
Stephanie Aird updated her status.
ooh and i havn't had a drink since Sunday,
think ill have a lil tipple (for medicinal
purposes ofcourse, on account of me wooden
legs).

Monday, 17 January 2011 at 18:58 UTC
Stephanie Aird updated her status.
FFS ran to answer the house phone, dropping
my last precious ryvita on the way and it was
the national WILL writing service asking if i
wanted to start a WILL, i said yes, start with
WILL and end it with f@ckoff.

Monday, 17 January 2011 at 18:01 UTC
Stephanie Aird updated her status.
Laugh and the world laughs with you. Cry and
you cry alone. Have a few stellas then ya wont
give a f@ck who does what :)

Monday, 17 January 2011 at 18:07 UTC
Stephanie Aird updated her status.
Gym -1 Alcohol- 0 my premier league score for
today.

Thursday, 10 February 2011 at 18:49 UTC
Stephanie Aird updated her status.
well its gettin' late, time to get me eyebrows
off, me falsies on, me pulin' pants out and me
snoggin' teeth in.

Saturday, 15 January 2011 at 18:43 UTC
Stephanie Aird updated her status.
slim fast half price in boots! Got me months
shoppin' in for 9 quid. (well 49 quid after i got
me stella in).

Friday, 14 January 2011 at 21:24 UTC
Stephanie Aird updated her status.
FFS, gonads of a sea cucumber and eating them
are an actual topic of a television programme.
Think ive had a bad bottle of stella,
hallucinating.bollox.

Friday, 14 January 2011 at 17:48 UTC
Stephanie Aird updated her status.
Day 10: change of scenery while excercising, no
gym (ill have withdrawel symptoms later) but
did go jogging with the dog (not to be confused
with dogging).

Thursday, 6 January 2011 at 17:05 UTC
Stephanie Aird updated her status.
as if its friday tomorrow already, not sure im
ready to drink again yet, ill just have to apply
myself more.

Friday, 31 December 2010 at 15:27 UTC
Stephanie Aird updated her status.
AS IF i cant hear shark tale for the baby
snoring, FFS :)

Thursday, 30 December 2010 at 21:24 UTC
Stephanie Aird updated her status.
10,9,8,7,6,5,4,3,2,1 happy
new.................hangover cos yav just drank
the special offer 10 pack stella from morrisons.

Thursday, 30 December 2010 at 16:42 UTC
Stephanie Aird updated her status.
ya know its time to consider swallowing
something sollid when ya start to shite stella.

Tuesday, 28 December 2010 at 22:06 UTC
Stephanie Aird updated her status.
my gift is my song and this ones for you. Ya
should hav seen every f@ckers face on
christmas mornin' when i handed out that
prezzie.

Friday, 24 December 2010 at 18:00 UTC
Stephanie Aird updated her status.
ya know its scarily cold when ya nipples are
ACTUALLY stuck to the windscreen while ya
driving.
Wednesday, 22 December 2010 at 18:10 UTC
Stephanie Aird updated her status.
ya know its cold when ya teeth are chatterin in
the glass on the bedside table.

Stephanie Aird updated her status.
might have to give the gym a rest tomorrow,
been every day since Sunday and me legs are
killin', feel like they're made of b@stard birch
(thats wood to all of us MDF junkies) :)

Stephanie Aird updated her status.
life is all that and some. (we know its not like
that all the time so grab all that when ya
can).

Stephanie Aird updated her status.
ya know its cold when ya can hang ya wasing
on ya nipples.

Stephanie Aird updated her status.
hell is hanging over me. Who invented alcohol
theyre taking the pissed.

Stephanie Aird updated her status.
it comes to somethin' when ya tweenager has
reached that stage in her life where a
computer screen and social network sites are
far more entertaining and important than the
person who gave birth to her. Ironically look
who im telling about it.

Wednesday, 10 November 2010 at 20:11 UTC
Stephanie Aird updated her status.
come on admit it, Sobo has made a fcn class
version of Perfect Day, Lou Reed must be
laughin all the way to the bank, or his dealer.

Wednesday, 10 November 2010 at 20:07 UTC
Stephanie Aird updated her status.
fuck me (urghh not like that) is Vorderman on
stilts?

Wednesday, 10 November 2010 at 18:58 UTC
Stephanie Aird updated her status.
teacher to topless, fire eating, lap dancing
hooker. If carlsberg did career changes.

Friday, 5 November 2010 at 11:22 UTC
Stephanie Aird updated her status.
Seeing the Beauty in Small Things.

Thursday, 4 November 2010 at 19:17 UTC
Stephanie Aird updated her status.
sckollob.

Sunday, 31 October 2010 at 20:27 UTC
Stephanie Aird updated her status.
errr, why is my white dog pink, bloody
tweenagers and fake blood. And me cushion
covers, arrrrgghhhh. Fcn halloween. Worth it
for the ket tho.

Stephanie Aird updated her status.
booked drummin' lessons for me betweenager,
seemed like a good idea, however, on second
thoughts.............i can only imagine where ill
end up sticking the fcn drum sticks.

Stephanie Aird updated her status.
the penny for the guy beggers as tesco express
accept cheques, charrrrrrrmin'.

Stephanie Aird updated her status.
Grandchildren a gift from God, Children, OM
fcn G.

Stephanie Aird updated her status.
cubborn stunt!

Stephanie Aird updated her status.
WTF, got an email like most of you probably
have selling life cover, with the opening line of
"if you were to die who would pay your bills".
Hellllloooooo, if am dead i wont have any bills,
how much gas, water and electric does a fcn
corpse need.

Friday, 24 September 2010 at 08:39 UTC+01
Stephanie Aird updated her status.
the pain in my throat is kiiiiiiling me, ouch. I
must talk too much at school, sign language it
is then from monday, good job i have lots of
interesting signs.

Saturday, 18 September 2010 at 17:29 UTC+01
Stephanie Aird updated her status.
now i know where dragons den rejects go to sell
their shitty products, ASDA, flash power mop,
WELLFCNAYE, worra load of bollocking shite!
Power mop my arse. Lmthinao.

Saturday, 18 September 2010 at 15:38 UTC+01
Stephanie Aird updated her status.
if i had a text to answer my thumbs wouldnt be
up to mischief, you know i have thumb
tourettes, bollox, wank, twat, SEE!

Tuesday, 31 August 2010 at 18:46 UTC+01
Stephanie Aird updated her status.
became a fan of: limber up ya thumbs ya slow
textin' kunt.

Thursday, 26 August 2010 at 14:21 UTC+01
Stephanie Aird updated her status.
where does the delicacy shit with sugar on
originate, cos according to me nana we were
having it for tea every night. Oddly enough its
what im making everytime anyone asks what
am cookin'.

Jesus me fingers are red raw with typing AND Ian's sat in the other room with some fucking bloke film on, FULL BASTARD BLAST, ya' know with loads of gun fire and shouting and shite....................................

The Last few pages of bits of this and bobs of that are coming up.....

I'm gonna have a comfort break (coffee and a shite) I'll be back in ten........

<u>Videography</u>-YouTube Links

Tesco Express – bitl.ly/2iBjoRx

Trolls Think Before Ya Type – bit.ly/2iBjs42

My Run In With Donald Trump –
bit.ly/2hqHUr2

Female Chubby Brown – bit.ly/2huhWV9

Stuck! – bit.ly/2iBv9Yn

Ian Is Doing My Titends In – bit.ly/2iBA9fv

Highlighting And Contouring –
bit.ly/2iolchN

Highlighting And Contouring (Continued) –
bit.ly/2ibwLcl

Cheeky Biatch Bastard – bit.ly/2i4x4aR

A Rock Chicks Fannies – bit.ly/2iojE7e

Unbelievable!! – bit.ly/2ieCSiB

Sundays With Ian – bit.ly/2hlxoOj

Petrol Station Weekly Excitement – bit.ly/
2iezxQD

It's Not Really Theft – bit.ly/2iotfeq

Dogs!!! – bit.ly/2ibA6YH

What Is It With Men And Boobs? –
bit.ly/2iBOHl9

4ft 2in Guinea Pigs – bit.ly/2i4CaUA

Low Fat Egg Sandwich – bit.ly/2i4EjQO

Have I missed anything out, I've never wrote a book before is there anything legal I have to put in, I havnt a fucking clue.

Oh wait don't I have to say summit like, any similarities to anyone living or dead in this book is purely coincidental apart from the alive and dead people I have mentioned. Aww fuck it i dunno how it goes. Id ask Ian but I might aswell talk to a punnet of mushrooms.

OOOh ive just looked in Justin Biebers paperback (no it's not mine FFS) to see what he has and apart from a load of bollox (pretty much like mine really) he's got links and stuff in....well if it's good enough for Justin Bieber its good enough for me.............................

Follow me on these if ya' dont already and if ya' want to ofcourse. Oh and please subscribe to me YouTube, cheers xxx

www.facebook.com/
Stephanie.aird1

https://m.youtube.com/
user/MsSaird

www.twitter.com/
StephAird

www.instagram.com/
Stephanieairdx

oooh that font looks a bit big, oh well I have a lot of silver surfing followers theyll be able to see it.

Thank you so much for buying my book. I am overwhelmed by the amount of support I am receiving from every one of You. You truly are the most amazing fans I could wish for, here is to many more years with you.

Big Thanks To:

All Of My Amazing Phannies,

To Fucking Ian-Drives mad but also anywhere my heart desires.....

My Humour, musical ability and strength of character is a blend of all my family and many friends I have met over the years.

My Daughters Robyn and She who will not be named-they both constantly wind me but they came to my first shows....heckled me all the way through but hey ho.....

My Mam-when I wanted to play an instrument she bought me a guitar, when I wanted to sing she bought me a tape recorder, when I told her I wanted to be a teacher she told me to go for it, when I told her I wanted to be a writer she bought me a pen-I love you Mam xxxxx

My Nana and Granda-I miss you both so much My Twisted Sister Hayley-she encourages me all the way with her contagious laughter xxx

My Neice Ellie-watches all of my videos, how cool is that xxx

Fern Duggan-a lovely girl I havnt even met but she has done so many wonderful things to support me and my page-thank you x

Callum Nicholson-This kid is going places I can tell ya' that!!!

My book buddy-Al Devon (he gets me bookings and many other things)-We met and lit the touch paper, we're both standing back to watch the fire together x

A special thanks to Bob Fischer of BBC Introducing for playoing my songs/pieces-You made believe I am a real musician xxx

A huge thank you to ALL of the friends that have been supportive on this strange journey-

But mainly to Joanne and Jason Boyle being the main instigators and urging me to go on. For being there ALWAYS-Thank you xxx

and to Book Publishers BLURB their Book Wright Tools are bloody Brilliant!!!

2014 was a bit dodgy when I first started making my videos, getting suspended, leaving my job etc.

2015 was proper canny, started my own business etc

2016 has been fcn class, I dont need to tell you, you were all there going through it with me.......

2017 is GONNA BE FCN MINT!

let me see what is there......
I'm on Judge Rinder In January
Launching my new website
Planning my nartionwide tour
starting my very own chat show
filming the new sitcom EXTRA EXTRA
making our own sitcom with Danny Posthill- love him, he's class.
Year round shows and events at my cafe-bar- shoppe, 55 Church, Street, Hartlepool

Writing more songs, making more videos and writing more books oh and crafting ofcourse x and many many other things, yaaaaaaay xxx

I think thats all for now, I'm starting the next book soon and also gonna do one with my songs and crafts in etc :)

Its 18:04pm On Wednesday 28th December 2016, i'm still in my Pjs as I've been working on this all day, i'm gonna get washed and dressed and that will take me to Cava O'Clock.......
I'll be back in my next book cos I have tons of stuff to tell ya' and ofcourse I'll be around in my videos, shows and all of that.

All the Best for 2017......

Dream big, chase hard, love lots and LAUGH LOADS........

LOVE YOU

BYE
xxxx

LOVE YOU

BYE

xxx

Lightning Source UK Ltd.
Milton Keynes UK
UKOW05f0817150317
296657UK00001B/9/P